The Image Makers

THE IMAGE MAKERS
Sixty Years of Hollywood Glamour

Text by Paul Trent

Designed by Richard Lawton

BONANZA BOOKS
New York

MCMLXXII by Paul Trent and Richard Lawton
All rights reserved.
This 1982 edition is published by Bonanza Books,
distributed by Crown Publishers, Inc.
by arrangement with McGraw Hill Book Company
Manufactured in Italy by A. Mondadori, Verona
ISBN: 0-517-376008

They took the blossoms of the oak, and the blossoms of the broom, and the blossoms of the meadow-sweet, and produced from them a maiden, the fairest and most graceful that man ever saw.

—from a fourteenth century Welsh manuscript

Contents

Dedication

This book is conceived in the hope that the works of many fine artists—namely, the Hollywood portrait photographers—will not be entirely lost to this and future generations. We have been guided in the selection of photographs by a wish to include only the most successful among the portraits available to us. We hope this collection exhibits the imagination and skill which many of these photographers achieved and will thus re-direct attention to their long-ignored talents.

The Image Makers

Glamour. 1. a magic spell: BEWITCHMENT 2. an elusive mysteriously exciting and often illusory attractiveness that stirs the imagination and appeals to a taste for the unconventional, the unexpected, the colorful, or the exotic: a strangely alluring atmosphere of romantic enchantment: a bewitching, intangible, irresistibly magnetic charm: personal charm and poise combined with unusual physical and sexual attractiveness.

from Webster's Third New International Dictionary
© 1971

"Glamour" has so strongly characterized Hollywood movies over the past sixty years that the two have come to be regarded as virtually synonymous. This fact is easily understandable, considering the extent to which audience taste dictates to the economics of movie-making. Certainly, if audiences did not support the Hollywood brand of glamour at the box office, it would not have been manufactured.

As defined above, glamour depends upon deception for achieving its effects. Technically, the motion picture is also dependent upon deception. The brain is deceived into believing that a series of rapidly projected, slightly different *still* photographs are actually moving pictures. The mind perceives an *illusion* of motion. For many this is far more "real" than the crunch of popcorn or uncomfortable seats.

An important part of this illusion is glamour. It is basic to the appeal of movies, for while films provide a popular form of entertainment, they are equally desirable as a form of escape. Many people are able to forget completely the painful and depressing realities of their daily lives by going to a movie. Hollywood, in fact, once advised Americans to "Get More Out of Life. Go Out to a Movie!"

With these deceptions so easily accomplished, it is not surprising that the actors who have been photographed and projected on a screen hundreds of sizes larger than life are able to bewitch so completely that audiences have attributed superhuman qualities to them. They have gone beyond the reality of being flesh-and-blood people acting out a story on the screen. They have become objects of fantasy. They have been lifted to a position so removed from earth that they have been called, appropriately, "stars."

The success or failure of any star ultimately rests with the audience. Newspaper copy has frequently created stars, but it has always taken audience support at the box office to sustain their careers. Stars do not appeal to an audience exclusively through the glamour of their personality and appearance. The roles they play are equally important to their continued popularity.

One of the most popular and powerful stars to emerge in the early days of the movies was Mary Pickford. She was one of several stars between the years 1915 and 1917 to earn a larger salary in one year than President Woodrow Wilson himself. Through the strength of her audience appeal and her popularity, Miss Pickford enjoyed a power in bargaining with the heads of studios that no star has enjoyed since. Her contract with Adolph Zukor in 1916 was an example of this extraordinary power. It provided that . . .

> . . . Miss Pickford could reject the *finished picture,* a privilege not granted since; a studio must be built for her, she must own it herself so no one else could make a movie there.
> The newspapers, in a state of shock, headlined the financial agreement:
>
> $1,400,000 a year salary.
> 50 percent of the profits of all Mary Pickford pictures.
>
> As president of the Mary Pickford Corporation, with her mother Charlotte as all the vice-presidents, she was to get, besides a $10,000 *a week* drawing account:
>
> $300,000 bonus for signing (also a first).
> A private car attached to any train if she traveled.
> Two limousines, chauffeurs paid by the studio, on call day and night.
> Her wardrobe in toto *on and off* the screen.
> Two maids both at the studio and at home.
>
> She had been off Zukor's payroll for four weeks while she considered offers from every other picture company and from industrial billionaires who wanted to form companies for her. She now made Zukor pay her $40,000 a week for those four weeks.

—from Adela Rogers St. Johns' *The Honeycomb,* Doubleday, 1969, pg. 158

The secret of Mary Pickford's bargaining power was simple. She was "America's Sweetheart." She was the first genuine movie star and her climb to that position was carefully planned and executed. She was a shrewd businesswoman who knew the importance of audience support to her continued popularity. Because they loved her as the "innocent" of such films as *Poor Little Peppina* and *Poor Little Rich Girl* she made this kind of role her specialty. The photograph (page 13) by the Evans Studio around 1915 perfectly captures the image which "Little Mary" maintained throughout most of her career.

In these early film days, stars were able to complete as many as three or four films a month, sometimes more. As a result, audiences got to know them as personalities rather quickly. This familiarity developed into a feeling of intimacy which audiences wanted to extend beyond the confines of the movie theatre. Large segments of the movie-going public began to write letters, postcards and to send telegrams to the stars. There was a continuing flow of mail from around the world to the Hollywood studios and the stars. The mail would contain proposals of marriage, recipes, advice on makeup and hairstyles, and upon occasion threats against the star's life. Such intensity of feeling and determination earned movie audiences a special name, "fans," short for "fanatic."

The job of seeing that fan mail is answered has traditionally belonged to the star's home studio, since very few stars have ever personally assumed responsibility for the enormous task of answering this bulk of mail. The most popular form of response to fan mail has been the autographed photograph of the star commonly called a "fan photo." Secretaries, employed to do little more than answer the fan mail, often autograph the photographs in the star's name.

Among the specialists employed to publicize stars and their films are photographers, layout designers, copy writers, and publicity executives. The photographers who are employed by the studios for supplying promotional material are known as "still men." They usually specialize in either "portrait" or "set" photography. Portrait work is done in special galleries designed for taking glamour portraits, while the set men are assigned to the movie sets where they take scene stills. Basically, the glamour portrait artist has three major concerns: maintaining the artistic and technical standards of his profession; supplying photographs which the studio needs for promotion; and capturing the basic qualities which support the star "image" of his subjects.

In tracing the developments in portrait photography from 1910 to 1970, it is interesting to notice the sameness of look which characterizes portraits of each decade. Naturally, the many technical advancements in the field of photography contribute to many observable changes in quality and technique. However, another factor may also be noted. The types of star images which prevail in each decade have had much in common. There has been a tendency to copy, or to be heavily influenced by the more successfully established and proven star images. The trend has limited the number of *original and unique* images which emerge in each decade. There are many stars who make the transition successfully from one decade to the next, but never without some obvious changes in image.

From about 1912 through the early Twenties, portrait photographers were rarely full-time studio employees. They were usually independents who main-

Mary Pickford, 1915

tained private galleries away from the studio, although upon occasion they might photograph the star on the movie set or at home. However, from the mid-Twenties until the early Fifties, each studio employed its own staff of portrait photographers and provided them large galleries in which to photograph the stars. Since the mid-Fifties the studios have, in general, returned to the practice of employing free-lance cameraman for special assignments.

In the decade before 1920, photography suffered not only from poor techniques but from limitations of the medium itself. The film used at the time was orthochromatic. It did not register colors correctly and was completely insensitive to red. Mouths came out black. Lighting was also crude. In most instances it was flat and unimaginative. Photographers seemed to have just about all they could manage lighting indoor subjects brightly enough to register on the film. Lights were usually placed directly in front of the subject and very little was done to model facial structure and body contours or to get details in shadows through proper placement of lights and with more careful exposure. Outdoor photography was also characterized by an inability to control light. Most photographs look very high in contrast, with few gradations between lights and darks. There is also a fuzziness resulting from a fondness for the soft-focus lens which characterizes most photographs.

Among the most popular stars of 1910 to 1920 were Mary Pickford, Charles Chaplin, Clara Kimball Young, the Gish sisters, Richard Barthelmess and Theda Bara. Their images tended to be characterized by a wholesomeness, and a down-to-earth quality. Even Theda Bara's "Vamp" was never particularly sophisticated in its representation of evil and wickedness. Because of the simplistic morality which characterized the plots of the early films, it was only natural that the star images would be as simple as the characters they played. Influenced as it was by the carry-over of Victorian attitudes and values, society at this time would never have tolerated images which were anything but moral and pure.

During the 1920s, the emphasis in photography began to shift away from the simplicity of the teens to a more extensive use of costumes and draping; to more involved and elaborate backgrounds. Lighting became more dramatic, and photographers began to use light to shape facial features and body contours. They were also learning more about getting details in shadows. Makeup was still generally heavy and orthochromatic film continued to be used. However, the soft focus was not as popular as it had been formerly. Overall, photographers demonstrated far more skill and imagination in their work.

The stars of the Twenties were far more sophisticated than had been their predecessors. The flappers, sheiks, swashbucklers, love gods and goddesses presented a strong contrast to the gentler tramps and Pollyannas of the preceding decade. The innocence of the earlier stars seemed all the more striking when contrasted with the worldly and wicked images of top stars like Greta Garbo,

Sincerely. Mary Pickford.

John Gilbert, Rudolph Valentino, Gloria Swanson, John Barrymore, Clara Bow and Marion Davies. These trend-setters managed to stay far out in front of everyone else in the frenetic society of the Jazz Age. Ironically, enjoying continued popularity alongside these stars were Mary Pickford and the Gish sisters, their images of innocence still very much intact. However, even "America's Sweetheart" fell victim to the changing times when in June of 1928 her long curls fell on a barber's floor in Chicago. She had finally decided to play "grown-up romances." Undoubtedly audience opinion had influenced this drastic change.

In 1927 the motion-picture industry was revolutionized by the success of "talking" pictures. For many of the silent screen stars this meant oblivion. John Gilbert is the most often mentioned actor who failed to make the transition from the silents to the talkies. His somewhat thin, tenor voice was a jarring contrast to his darkly handsome, romantic looks. His image had been that of the mysterious, Latin lover; his voice suggested something entirely different. This is not to imply he would not have been an effective actor in talking pictures. It more pointedly illustrates the power of an audience to determine the success or failure of any star. Audiences were simply unwilling to accept John Gilbert in a new light.

A second event which was to affect the motion-picture industry during the Twenties was also to affect the entire nation as well. The crash of the stock market in 1929 threw the entire country into panic. The beginning of the great depression signaled the changing of a country's values, its priorities and its styles of living. There was never a greater need for the escape which movies could provide than during the depression years of the Thirties.

Photographers of the Thirties, imaginative and tasteful, were responsible for bringing many positive values to the art of portrait photography. The photography reflects an increased awareness of the effects of contrasting lights and shadows. More attention is paid to creating shapes and mood through the placement of lights around the subject. Photographers began to make numerous creative uses of the camera, such as Clarence S. Bull's exquisite photography of Garbo using a single light source, and the marvelous effects achieved by Elmer Fryer and Scotty Welbourne with multiple exposures.

Technically, the development of panchromatic film gave photographers the opportunity to achieve more control over their work. This film gave greater accuracy in shades of color, and was sensitive to red. Lips no longer appeared to be quite so black. There was still evidence of soft focus being preferred by some, but that remains true today.

During the depression, movies which could talk and sing and dance—and be heard doing it—were making Americans' lives a bit more tolerable. There was a need in every walk of life for the kind of temporary escape which the movies could provide. Fan mail came pouring into the studios between 1930 and 1935 in excess of 32 million letters a year. Publicity and advertising departments were forced to increase their staffs just to handle the fan mail and to send out fan photos. Fan clubs were also growing in size and number. These "devoted fanatics" of Hollywood glamour were finding pleasure through a total immersion in the magic of the movie stars.

Numerous new stars were created during the depression. Many of them like Jean Harlow, Clark Gable, Barbara Stanwyck and Robert Taylor were typical of the most glamorous stars. Others like Paul Muni, James Cagney and Edward G. Robinson represented a new breed of star. Audiences seemed to respond to these personalities because they recognized them as being closer to themselves, as more "real" and human, as being untouched by glamour. However, by standards of "real" in the Sixties, these stars would also appear to be very glamorous, although certainly not so much so as Jean Harlow.

Many of the stars who had been popular during the silent days had been able to change their images sucessfully and to keep audience favor during the Thirties. Some, like Joan Crawford, Greta Garbo, Norma Shearer, Ronald Colman and Gary Cooper simply became more glamorous. Comedy star Charles Chaplin, however, regarded the talking picture as simply unthinkable. He is said to have commented in 1922 that sound would ruin the motion picture as surely as "painting statuary. I would as soon rouge marble cheeks. There would be nothing left to the imagination," he said. Still, Chaplin was popular whenever he made a film, although after 1928 he made two films, *City Lights* in 1931 and *Modern Times* in 1936, which were silent except for a musical background. Not until 1940 did he make his first talking film, *The Great Dictator.*

The Thirties have often been regarded as the era of the fan magazine. During this period they grew not only in number but expanded in size to the point where *Photoplay* in 1937 was of the same dimensions as *Esquire.* The number of subscriptions also reached new highs, and the newsstand sales were impressive enough to encourage one hopeful publisher to issue a "quality" film magazine selling for 50 cents a copy as compared to the other magazines which sold for no more than 15 cents a copy, some as low as 5 cents. (It was called *Cinema Arts,* and lasted for four issues.) Each month the latest portraits taken in Hollywood were printed in special gallery sections of the fan magazines, and the fans came to regard this as their most inexpensive and dependable source of photographs of their favorite stars.

The power which the fan magazines had in the star-making process did not go unrecognized by the studios. In fact, they *used* the magazines to reach their audience—a relatively inexpensive form of publicity and advertising. The studio publicity departments maintained constant communication with the magazine editors. They would send representatives to the magazine offices regularly to show editors the most recent portraits taken by the studio photographers. In many instances, one magazine would compete with another to get exclusive rights for first-time publication of portraits of the most popular stars like Garbo, Gable and Crawford. This cooperation between studio and publisher can only be regarded as a partnership in the marketing of glamour. It was undoubtedly a lucrative one.

About 1936, the portrait photographers began to be elevated to star status in the fan magazines. Articles began to appear regularly during the next few years focusing attention on the portrait photographer as an artist in his own right. One such article appeared in *Photoplay* in June, 1938, devoting several pages to the work of George Hurrell, who at that time was working as a free-lance photographer. The article described Mr. Hurrell as a "brilliant pioneer in the modern camera field, who, through his own genius, established the reputation that today sometimes insures him as much as $1000 for a single sitting." Hurrell's technical success was said to be the "result of inspired use of lighting; specifically in his ability to create a mood and then, in one perfect moment, to record it. To this artist, the preliminary of arousing enthusiasm in the subject is requisite —a process that may involve, on his part, a song, a joke, even a jig or two. The results—dramatic studies of individual types of glamour, each alive with light and shadow." The article further suggested that Hurrell, by "rebelling against the rigid rules of 'still' photography, has combined the warmth of the painter's art with the cold precision of the cameraman's skill. Thus, he has been successful in capturing in his portraits both the fluid beauty of his glamorous subjects and all the subtle nuances of their personalities." Perhaps the most novel assertion in the article is that "the secret of Hurrell's magic lies in the fact that each picture is taken to musical accompaniment. In the studio, a record plays constantly, its music varied to the mood of the subject. Thus, for [photographing] Luise Rainer, a waltz; for Shirley Temple, a lullaby."

While the fan magazines were giving the Hollywood portraitists special attention on a regular basis, the more fashionable magazines such as *Vanity Fair, Vogue* and *Harper's Bazaar* were practically ignoring their work. Instead, the editors were sending independent photographers such as Alfred Eisenstaedt, Cecil Beaton, Nickolas Muray, Hoyningen-Huene and Edward Steichen to Hollywood to photograph the stars in their homes or on studio lots and sets.

Actually, there may be several reasons why the work of the Hollywood cameramen did not satisfy the editors of the chic magazines. As photographers, their specialization in portraiture of the stars was probably one factor against them. Had they been freer to work with a number of more diversified subjects as did Beaton, Steichen and Eisenstaedt, perhaps they would have found greater interest expressed in their work. Or perhaps the studio's publicity department did not consider those magazines a valuable source of publicity, since their circulations were low by comparison to those of the fan magazines. Consequently, studios probably did not care to plant the so-called "exclusive" or more exciting examples of studio photography with "class" magazines.

Each of the Hollywood studios had its own outstanding portrait photographers with handsomely equipped galleries in which to work. Metro-Goldwyn-Mayer had Clarence S. Bull. He had joined the studio in the year of its formation, when it was advertising that it had "More Stars Than There Are in Heaven" under contract. Some of those stars were Greta Garbo, John Gilbert, John Barrymore and Joan Crawford. Bull photographed them all. He was with the studio from the early Twenties until his retirement in 1955. He writes in his book, *The Faces of Hollywood*, of discovering the most effective method of lighting Jean Harlow's platinum-blond hair—other photographers had found it difficult to capture without making her look cheap and overdone. Bull used a surgeon's lamp which he and Harlow "lifted" from a movie set because it could be aimed and focused with more flexibility than the other lights in his studio.

RKO-Radio Pictures Studio's top photographer for better than twenty-five years was Ernest A. Bachrach. He was responsible for practically all the glamour portraits taken of Katharine Hepburn during the Thirties while she was the studio's top female star.

Paramount Studio's top photographer was Eugene Robert Richee. When he arrived at the studio in 1923, Rudolph Valentino was at the peak of his popularity. He also was the first photographer to pose Gary Cooper for portraits as well as other important stars at Paramount like Marlene Dietrich, Claudette Colbert, Ida Lupino, Ann Sheridan, Susan Hayward and Carole Lombard. Several other outstanding portraitists joined Richee in the Paramount gallery over the years. These included Kenneth Alexander, William Walling, Jr., Irving Lippman, Otto Dyar and Don English.

At Warner Brothers Studio, where almost as many stars were under contract as there were at M-G-M, the top photographers were Elmer Fryer and Scotty Welbourne. Between them they took hundreds of thousands of portraits of stars like Bette Davis, Olivia de Havilland, James Cagney, Kay Francis, Paul Muni, John Garfield, Joan Blondell, Ruby Keeler, Dick Powell, Humphrey Bogart, Edward G. Robinson and Errol Flynn.

At Columbia Studios, A. L. "Whitey" Schafer, William Fraker and Carl DeVoy were the top photographers in the Thirties. They photographed such stars as Ronald Colman, Margo, Carole Lombard, Irene Dunne, Cary Grant and Jean Arthur.

At Fox Studios (which became 20th Century-Fox in 1935), the photographs for publicity were furnished by Max Munn Autry, Hal Phyfe and Alexander Kahle. The stars they photographed included Janet Gaynor, Charles Farrell,

George O'Brien, Alice Faye, Shirley Temple, Joel McCrea and Claire Trevor.

Intense plotting and scheming by actors and actresses to steal successfully proven Hollywood "images" can be traced back to the earliest silent days. Numerous aspiring actresses hoped to replace Mary Pickford in little girl roles and assume her title of America's Sweetheart, and practically every starlet (even some first rank stars) posed in vamp costumes to cash in on the popularity of Theda Bara's image. Neither these efforts, nor the painfully obvious ones made in the Twenties by male actors hoping to replace Valentino, can compare to the machinations Hollywood witnessed when Paramount Studio launched its campaign to dethrone the mighty Garbo at M-G-M. Their candidate was Marlene Dietrich, the star of their German import, *The Blue Angel*. The studio announced her arrival in this country with her director and mentor Joseph von Sternberg as the end of Garbo's reign! The plot backfired spectacularly. Dietrich's image was so uniquely her own that she became the star other studios tried to copy. Even at Paramount the starlets were forced to pay tribute to the Dietrich allure. Her special brand of glamour was held as a new ideal, and all the young ladies were, at one time or another, given makeup and hairdos and gowns similar to those worn by Dietrich. They were then asked by the portrait photographers to strike poses similar to the ones assumed by Dietrich, who, through her close association with von Sternberg, had learned about camera techniques as well as about lighting and composition. She quite possibly would have been a talented director in her own right. She had been molded just as had hundreds of other stars. But she was different in that she *understood* glamour and how it worked. She was intelligent enough to participate in the creation of her image.

There were many attempts to copy Dietrich, just as other top stars were copied—Crawford, Swanson, Harlow and Garbo, to mention but a few. As late as 1939, Paramount was willing to invest in a Dietrich look-alike, Isa Miranda, to star in a film which Dietrich had started in 1936 and abandoned after costing the studio some $900,000. At that time she had just been named by theatre owners across the country as box-office poison, but by 1939 she was at Universal Studios starring in the successful film *Destry Rides Again*, and Paramount was ready to cash in on the power of her particular glamour appeal.

The portraits (page 20) illustrate vividly the changes which stars underwent in an effort to capitalize upon proven box-office images. Miriam Hopkins, under contract to Paramount in the early Thirties, was posed by studio photographers in a variety of moods. The 1932 portrait captures the mood and feeling of the famous Garbo portrait which Edward Steichen took and which appeared on the cover of *Life* magazine. The 1934 portrait is clearly an attempt to capture the look of Dietrich.

Carole Lombard was another player at Paramount who understood camera techniques and knew about lighting. Because of an accident which had scarred her face, Miss Lombard educated herself in the technical aspects of film-making. She knew how to pose as well as how to light a scene and where to place the camera for the most effective takes. She directed Alfred Hitchcock for his traditional walk-on scene in the 1941 film *Mr. and Mrs. Smith* in which she was the star.

Both Dietrich and Lombard knew when lights were properly placed. They knew if the camera had been properly angled and located. They knew if their makeup was correct for achieving a particular effect. They also knew how to wear clothes and how to present themselves most attractively for the camera, and there obviously was a similarity in their "look" (pages 22 and 23). The portraits of these two actresses by Eugene Robert Richee, William Walling, Jr., and Kenneth Alexander at Paramount during the Thirties may well be the most *consistently* successful portraits ever taken of any Hollywood stars. Better than 670 portraits were taken in Dietrich's stay at Paramount, while Lombard's portrait file contains well over 1700.

As the early stages of World War II were developing in Europe during the late Thirties, there was a noticeable change taking place in the glamour images in Hollywood. The more cosmetic, refined glamour such as was embodied by Dietrich and Lombard was giving way to a more natural look. Bette Davis was a popular star who effectively demonstrated the trend toward naturalness both in appearance and in the roles she played.

The Forties brought World War II to America and Hollywood. Studio portrait photographers were working overtime on what had formerly been called "leg art," only it was now being called the "pinup." The pinup was becoming an international institution thanks to all the empty barracks walls, and the most popular pinup girl of them all was Betty Grable. She was promoted as the "All-time Pinup Queen" and the servicemen's favorite pose of her was one taken by 20th Century-Fox photographer Frank Powolny in which she is in swimsuit, on tiptoe, looking over her shoulder into the camera. She and the studio mailed thousands of prints of the shot to servicemen and fans throughout the world.

Servicemen seemed to find in the pinup just the proper balance between the real (flesh) and the ideal (fantasy). They expressed a preference for "lots of flesh" in the pinups, but they also wanted the poses to be only suggestive of sex. In order to provide what the soldiers wanted, all the studios began to develop their pinup potential. Many starlets were kept under contract for no other purpose. During the war years, fan mail soared into the 60- and 70-million bracket as soldiers, teenagers, lonely housewives and fans of all descriptions all over the world requested pinups and portraits of their favorites. The circulation of fan magazines like *Photoplay* and *Modern Screen* reached their peak, and new magazines began to appear on the market. Because of advances in color

right Miriam Hopkins, 1932

below Miriam Hopkins, 1934

photography as well as in printing techniques, color photographs became a regular feature of fan magazines.

Columbia Picture's top photographer, Robert Coburn, in an interview appearing in *Popular Photography*, May, 1946, described the taking of pinup poses as a lengthy and complex process. "Before the picture is shot, the idea is sketched by an artist, and the prop and costume departments then work on costume and background. Once the preliminaries are over, I work very fast because I use few props—usually just one to symbolize the idea of the shot, such as a telephone, an overseas cap, a date book."

In addition to the pinup, photographers began to concentrate more on the candid photograph during the Forties. Fans wanted to see their favorite stars on USO tours or putting in time at the Hollywood Canteen. One of the first photographers to specialize in the candid was Paul Hesse. His candid portraits of the stars were featured monthly on the cover of *Photoplay* from the mid-Thirties until 1946. Hesse was outstanding as a color artist as well as with the traditional black-and-white. Along with the candids, there was still a continuing demand for glamour portraits taken in the studio galleries. And, as always, the studios responded to the demands of audiences. If they requested pinups, they received pinups. If it was portraiture or candids they preferred, they received those. The male stars were even photographed wearing their military uniforms. When a star decided what branch of the service he was entering, the photography department made certain he had a formal sitting in uniform before leaving for duty. These shots were usually printed in the fan magazines in articles directed at encouraging Americans to support the war effort.

Certainly the major publicity campaigns of the Forties were those which launched the careers of Veronica Lake and Jane Russell. The fact that neither actress was ever particularly praised for her acting skills makes the hullabaloo all the more fascinating. Each was given a promotional campaign such as Hollywood had not witnessed since the Garbo-Dietrich operation of the early Thirties.

Veronica Lake was presented by Paramount as a sultry, kittenish sex object who habitually leered and pouted behind a peek-a-boo bang. She once declared that the bang was definitely not a publicity gimmick. It was the result of the way her hair naturally fell. True or not, it was a natural for the publicity department. She was a *star* (if you believed the newspaper copy) before her second film was released. And the Paramount portrait photographers played a vital part in the creation of her very marketable image. In fact, if the portrait photographer has ever been responsible for the *creation* of any star's image, it was in the case of Veronica Lake. Once seen in still portraits, she gained nothing when seen in motion on the screen. The portrait photographers were able to capture her appeal in its entirety in the flat, two-dimensional portraits which had her loung-

opposite Carole Lombard, 1937

Marlene Dietrich, 1932

Veronica Lake, 1945

ing in sequined gowns or snuggling up to the head of a leopard (page 24).

Jane Russell's career was engineered by Howard Hughes, who employed top publicist Russell Birdwell and later the forces of the RKO publicity and photo departments in an effort to create the most sensational star in the history of films. She was posed as a lusty, carnal and earthy creature who seemed to reside most frequently in haystacks (page 27). Even when her first film, *The Outlaw,* was held up by the censors for three years, she received over 1100 fan letters each week for the entire period. Her popularity was sustained entirely by publicity photographs. A press release of 1942 announced that "better than 43,000 different photographs have been distributed of Jane Russell!"

Rita Hayworth also rocketed to stardom during the war years. Although her success appeared to be the usual overnight Hollywood rags-to-riches story, in reality she had been in films since the mid-Thirties. As Rita Cansino, she was under contract to Fox Studios but made little progress. When she moved to Columbia Studios her roles remained small and mostly forgettable until she was loaned back to 20th Century-Fox in 1941 for their remake of *Blood and Sand*. Cast as the fiery seductress who lured Tyrone Power into sin and destruction, she received critical and audience approval which the head of Columbia Studios, Harry Cohn, could not ignore. Cohn concentrated the energies of his publicity machinery on making Rita Hayworth the love goddess of the movies. Her most effective exposure was in the pages of *Life* magazine: one photograph in particular taken by *Life* photographer Bob Landry rivaled the popularity of Betty Grable's over-the-shoulder pose. The photograph shows Hayworth sitting in bed wearing a form-fitting negligee. A copy was supposedly taped to the bomb dropped on Hiroshima.

The list of stars who were able to change their images as the times changed remained long and impressive during the Forties. Former silent-screen stars like Gary Cooper, Joan Crawford and Ronald Colman were still popular, as were Bette Davis, Clark Gable, Rosalind Russell, Fred MacMurray, Marlene Dietrich, Judy Garland, Barbara Stanwyck and Robert Taylor, whose popularity had begun in the Thirties.

Throughout the Forties these stars were among the top money-makers at the box office. Audiences responded to the fact that they entertained the troops around the world, that they toured the country selling war bonds, and that they joined the military themselves (as in the cases of Robert Taylor and Clark Gable). These stars represent an ever-increasing tendency toward star images which more closely approximate "flesh" than had existed in any period before them. And as the 1940's came to an end, the star system which had produced fantasy images seemed destined to disappear before many more years had passed.

Jane Russell, 1943

During the 1950's the role of the portrait photographer underwent significant alterations. As film production began to decrease, as contract players became fewer, and as the major stars began to assert their independence, the number of still men employed by the studios began to dwindle. Their work also began to be unimaginative. It was neither new, original nor exciting. It might be best described as assembly-line. Stars were given the same lighting effects, their poses were relatively uniform and they were posed against the same backgrounds, portrait after portrait. Different stars would even pose against the same brick walls, the same painted backdrops. There was very little concern for individuality, and certainly there was very little photography that could be described as genuinely exciting.

The career of Marilyn Monroe began and flourished during this period of lack-lustre. Her popularity was chiefly sustained through the impact of her pinup poses, her most enthusiastic fans being the soldiers fighting the Korean War. If the pinup can be validly regarded as a major factor in sustaining the careers of stars during World War II, it was equally instrumental in supporting Monroe's climb to stardom. Soldiers kept the publicity department of 20th Century-Fox working overtime answering requests for pinups of her. Her stardom was achieved in a relatively short time, although she, like Rita Hayworth, had been working in films for five or six years before she began to approximate anything like stardom. During those early years, she had posed nude for a calendar, and the revelation of this was anything but detrimental to her popularity. The studio photographers posed her in everything from the standard bathing suit to a potato sack. She was always beautiful and magical even though, for a star of her importance, there were surprisingly few outstanding portraits or pinups taken of her by studio photographers. In fact, there were more exciting photographs taken of Monroe by photographers who were not affiliated with the studio than were taken by studio cameramen.

The Fifties also saw the emergence of a new form of entertainment—television. The impact of television on the motion-picture industry was initially felt most severely at the box office as attendance dropped off abruptly in the early months of 1951. The total effects are difficult to measure even today. Certainly television's immediacy, its live quality, had a tremendous effect on audiences, and interestingly, Hollywood's first reactions were to counter the loss by developing "gimmicks" it had shelved years earlier as impractical. 3-D was their first tactic, and this was quickly replaced by the giant screen effects of Cinemascope. Neither had strong enough appeal to bring millions out of their homes and back into the movie theatres. Audiences became younger. Those over twenty no longer seemed interested enough to turn off the television and hire a baby sitter or to take the children with them to the movies.

This became the decade of the rebel in Hollywood. Few stars had rebelled against the studio chieftains in the years since the mid-Thirties when Bette Davis walked out on Warner Brothers and went to England, in effect breaking a contract she thought was ruining her career. Bette Davis had lost, and for a long time few stars had dared to rebel. Still, in the 1950's it became fashionable to go on studio suspension. The more rigid the position taken by the studio against the stars' demands, the more determined the stars became to resist and break away from the hold of the studio contract.

The roles which best characterized the period were those of rebels. *Rebel without a Cause*, *The Wild Ones*, and *On the Waterfront* were but a few of the films in which the central character was a rebel, an anti-hero. He was outside society, fighting for his right to be himself. The films' stars, James Dean and Marlon Brando, were the epitome of the rebel. They were the perfect anti-heroes. Curiously, there were no women in this same category. If there has ever been one, it is probably Tuesday Weld, although she was a product of the 1960's. Basically, this entire decade of the Fifties is most easily identifiable by the feeling of anger and rebellion which so many of the popular stars' images projected.

Confidential magazine was another important influence on the movies in the Fifties. This magazine published scandalous revelations about the private lives of the stars, and was more popular at the newsstands than any of the fan magazines. In fact, *Confidential* was the forerunner in the change which began to occur in fan magazines around 1958. They began to turn their attention from the movie stars—who were admittedly diminishing in number due to the changes in the star system—toward the stars of television. The tone of the articles was no longer flattering to the stars, and more often than not, the titillating headlines of the stories had little to do with their contents. Actually, the strongest influence which *Confidential* exerted was to bring about the end of the glamour which had dominated the fan magazines for almost half a century. Ironically, however, it was also responsible for precipitating an inversion of glamour, or stimulating a change toward the glamour of ugliness. This anti-glamour was as vital to the appeal of James Dean and Marlon Brando (as anti-heroes) as glamour had been to the appeal of Marlene Dietrich and Carole Lombard (as goddesses of beauty).

While the anti-heroes (flesh) were enjoying increased popularity, there were still many young studio contract players who were already popular with the teenagers at the box office and who were being groomed to carry on glamour (fantasy) in the old Hollywood tradition. Under contract to the various studios were Debbie Reynolds, Elizabeth Taylor and Grace Kelly at M-G-M; Natalie Wood and Tab Hunter at Warner Brothers; Robert Wagner at 20th Century-Fox; and a large number of young players at Universal Studios. This group included

Rock Hudson, Tony Curtis, Jeff Chandler, Julie Adams, Scott Brady, Barbara Rush, Piper Laurie and Hugh O'Brian. Of these, Rock Hudson and Tony Curtis have come closest to achieving "star power" as it was enjoyed by Gable, Bogart and Cooper. With the exception of Jeff Chandler who died in 1961 and Piper Laurie who has retired, the others continue to be active in films and on television.

The major publicity campaign of the Fifties to create a new star was focused on Kim Novak. Columbia Studio's chief, Harry Cohn, was forced to find a replacement for his studio's wandering love goddess, Rita Hayworth. An article in *Playboy*, October, 1959, by Al Morgan recounts the story which begins with Hayworth walking out on Cohn, and continues with hisdeclaration that "so we don't have another dame with big boobs on the lot. So what? We ain't got a star? We'll make one!" A young starlet named Marilyn Novak was chosen as the product to be "processed" and "packaged." Her name was changed from Marilyn (to avoid confusion with Monroe), to Kit (which made her cry), to Kim. Just as had been the case with Jane Russell, Kim Novak was known to the American public as a movie star before she had appeared on screen in a major role. The thousands of stills, picture layouts and articles which appeared on her in the national magazines and fan magazines and Sunday supplements were responsible for her stardom.

While Kim Novak was being created to replace Rita Hayworth, Jayne Mansfield and Sheree North were being given huge build-ups in the magazines as replacements for Marilyn Monroe. (Monroe had also become a rebel and walked out on her contract at 20th Century-Fox.) In determining the proper image for Kim Novak, Harry Cohn saw her as being "something a little more subtle, a little more old-fashioned" than either Monroe or Mansfield. She was to be "the promissory note of sex. She was to purr where others growled. She was to be half bitch, half baby. She was to have a sexy sweetness, a virtuous voluptuousness."

To achieve this image photographically, two of Columbia's top photographers, Robert Coburn and his assistant, Cronenweth, placed Miss Novak in poses reminiscent of the portraiture of the early Thirties (page 31). This was an effective choice, since it re-inforced the roles she was soon to play in *The Eddy Duchin Story* and *Jeanne Eagles.* Each film was set in the late Twenties and early Thirties and the makeup and costuming styles complemented her platinum blonde image which was often compared to Jean Harlow's.

By 1962, the conflict between having to remain locked into the glamorous sex goddess image (which she had been created to play), and the need to rebel against it (which it was her natural inclination to do), left Marilyn Monroe dead of an overdose of sleeping pills at the age of thirty-six. Kim Novak remarked after Monroe's death that they had both felt themselves regarded by studio bosses as pieces of meat which had been wrapped up and sold across the counter. Miss Novak's career also suffered when she rebelled against Hollywood's glitter and made it clear that she preferred the seclusion and quiet of her ocean home.

During the Sixties, a completely different photographic concept prevailed. The publicity photograph was characterized primarily by the informal, unposed look of the candid. The *Blow-Up* photographer, who worked rapidly, frantically with his subject in an effort to penetrate deeply into the hidden recesses of personality and being, attempting to capture essence, is an effective prototype of the Sixties photographer. He works with faster film; smaller, more mobile cameras; greater physical freedom; and with a greater desire for capturing *fact* than an illusion of it. Photo journalism heavily influenced the work of still-photographers in the Sixties.

Of the old-guard photographers still active during the Sixties, George Hurrell was one of the more prominent. He was special portrait photographer for *Myra Breckenridge* late in 1969 and early in 1970 for 20th Century-Fox. Hurrell observed in January of 1970 that there were many regrettable changes to be found in the "new Hollywood." One being that "My gallery at the studio is all set up, but it's empty."

Among the stars of the Sixties, there was an obvious lack of interest in posing for portraits. Jerry Anderson, head of Fox's New York photo department, stated recently, "It is difficult to get the stars to pose for portraits these days. They don't want to spend the time." Certainly this is true of a great many stars. But why? The answer might be that today's audiences feel more comfortable with the anti-glamour of a Dustin Hoffman than with the more refined, glamorous qualities of a Rudolph Valentino. Interestingly, at the same time there is a resurgence of concern with nostalgia!

Another explanation for this preference for non-glamour is offered by Jack Kerness of Columbia Pictures Publicity Department. He feels that "the end of portrait photography came about not so much because the stars refuse to pose. Many of them would gladly do that. I blame it on the magazine editors. They don't want posed material, and I suppose they are dictated to by their readers. If they would print posed portraits, we would supply them. It's as simple as that." He stated further that his studio no longer thinks of the fan magazine as a useful outlet for the promotion of films or stars. "The movie magazines used to be powerful. Their circulation used to be tremendous, but today they seem to appeal to another kind of audience than moviegoers. They're more on Jackie Onassis than on movies and movie stars. We rarely even supply them with material."

Looking back to the definition of "glamour" which introduces this chapter, it would be difficult to support the contention that today's stars lack glamour. Barbra Streisand, Paul Newman, Robert Redford, Steve McQueen, Dustin

Hoffman, Raquel Welch and Elvis Presley are persons who "appear delusively magnified or glorified." Obviously they possess a kind of magic which attracts thousands whenever they appear publicly, and which makes their films guaranteed money-makers at box offices around the world. Certainly they are powerful enough to form their own production companies. They are rarely even referred to in print as just stars, rather as "superstars." Glamorous, powerful, popular though they are, there are relatively few exciting or even interesting still photographs to be found of any of them—with the possible exception of Raquel Welch, who has been rather effectively photographed by Terry O'Neill, and Barbra Streisand, who takes particular interest in the photography which is used of her in publicizing her films as well as television specials and record albums. (Streisand once recalled a record album because she was dissatisfied with the jacket.)

In retrospect, a scene which keeps coming to mind is one from Robert Aldrich's 1955 film *The Big Knife*, in which Jack Palance, playing a movie star in the old tradition, is forced to go to the still photographer's studio. There is no question that he feels only hatred, resentment and disgust toward the entire experience. Conceivably this same attitude was held by many stars of the past. Were their hours in the portrait gallery always pleasant? For many, they obviously were not. For others, clearly they were. Certainly there are millions of fans who valued and responded to that brand of glamour captured in the portraits, pinups and other publicity photographs of the past. For these people their disappearance has created a very real void. As for the stars today who seem on the surface to be outside the glamour picture, it is certain that they possess their own type of glamour appeal, and it would indeed add an additional dimension to their image to find them at least spending more time with still photographers.

The Images

Traditionally, studio photographers produced a variety of portraits ranging from the simplicity and formality of the "gallery" head-shot to the location or "at-home" candid. The objective was always to capture the stars in a glamorous mood whether they were posing in a costume on the set, relaxing in their own home, or modeling the latest fashions by studio designers. The definitions and photographs presented here should help to distinguish the various types of studio portraits.

I. *Gallery Portraits*

In these photographs, the subject is carefully lighted and posed while strict attention is paid to composition, form, line, gesture, movement and focus. The sitting usually takes place in the photographer's gallery, where formality in a photographic sense characterizes the work. Portraits are primarily for general publicity release and for distribution as fan photos.

The negatives for these and all photographs, whether still or portrait, are individually numbered, usually in the lower right-hand corner, and are kept by the studio in separate files for each star and film title. For portraits, the stars' initials are used followed by sequential numbering so that a portrait of Clark Gable numbered C.G.-32 would indicate portrait number 32 in his file of several hundred different shots.

There are generally seven types of gallery portraits:

    A. The standard head-shot (pages 44 and 45) —here the face is all-important. The star is posed simply so that with careful lighting the basic qualities of personality are effectively captured.

    B. The duo portrait (page 46) —frequently referred to as "two-shots." Two stars are posed together, usually in costume for a specific film. These photographs often have the look of a scene still, since they are usually taken on the set and are often suggestive of actual moments from the film.

    C. The costume portrait (pages 48 and 49) —these "head-shots" or full-length poses present the star in costume for a specific film. They may be taken in the photographer's gallery or on the set. Their primary usefulness is for advertising illustration.

    D. The fashion portrait (page 36) —in these the star is photographed modeling fashions by studio designers. Most frequently distributed to fan magazines for special fashion layouts, these portraits placed emphasis on

such items as dresses, suits, coats, hats, gowns, gloves, jewelry and shoes.
E. The pinup (pages 40 and 41). The focus here is on figure or physique
with the Greek concept of beauty, "nothing in excess," dominating. These
are often referred to as "beefcake" or "cheesecake."
F. The creative portrait (pages 35 and 37). Here the star is captured in
unusual poses which achieve their effect strictly in graphic terms. In each
the photographer's skill and imagination are more important than the
"star" qualities of his subject.
G. The "glamour" portrait (pages 50 and 51). These *special* portraits
represent glamour in its most concentrated form. They are the most carefully lighted and posed portraits taken by the studio photographers.
Capturing the star most glamorously is the objective in each.

II. *Candid Portraits.*

Candids are generally characterized by their informality of pose. Location is
also important, since stars are always photographed in natural surroundings
such as their homes, the movie set, at the swimming pool, the beach, attending
a premiere, or on location for a film. Candids are usually taken in available light,
thereby avoiding the artificiality of the gallery shot. There is also more *action*
associated with the candid. It never suggests the "hold-that-pose" feeling of
the strict glamour portrait.

Candids are usually published with "tags" such as "the star at home," "the
star on the set," "the star at the beach," or "the star at play" (pages 38, 39, 42,
43 and 47).

Ida Lupino, 1941

Norma Shearer, 1934

opposite James Cagney, 1942

opposite Richard Cromwell, 1934

left Clark Gable, 1935

below Claire Trevor, 1935

above Ramon Novarro, 1926

right George O'Brien, 1925

opposite Loretta Young, 1931

opposite Alice Brady, 1936

Elizabeth Taylor, 1963

opposite Claudette Colbert, 1935

Gilbert Roland, 1935

46

left Ward Bond and Gene Tierney, 1941

below Nelson Eddy and Jeanette MacDonald, 1937

opposite Jean Simmons, 1953

Yvonne De Carlo, 1947

Ida Lupino, 1941

opposite Ida Lupino and Scotty Welbourne, 1941

Reflections of the Stars

In the following interviews, four stars of the Hollywood screen reflect upon their careers as glamorous movie personalities and upon the portrait artists who photographed them during their many years of stardom. They also comment on portraits of themselves which are included in the "gallery" section of the book. (The interviews follow alphabetically.)

JOAN BLONDELL. New York, December, 1971.

It's fascinating that photographers wanted me to be as cute as apple pie one minute, and *sultry* the next. Well, *trying* to be sultry! During sittings they wanted many different angles, different attitudes, although most of them wanted me to smile, I think because my face lit up at that particular time in my life. You know, when you're young and beautiful and have great white teeth and all that. They'd say, "Come on, let's have that Blondell *smile!* There we *go! Got it!*

Ohhhhh. This portrait . . . seeing it just gave me chills. This was something important in my life because it was somebody's favorite picture who died. It was lost in a fire years ago. I thought I'd never see it again. And there it is (page 183). All during the Thirties, when I wasn't in front of a movie camera, I was in the gallery posing for portraiture. Also they'd have me out on location somewhere hanging onto a *tree.* Maybe leaning on a rock or something.

Elmer Fryer photographed me most during the Thirties. He did some great things of me. George Hurrell was fantastic, too. He was at Metro. And there was Clarence Bull at Metro. He did *lovely* things. I think the still gallery at Metro was the most careful. Their stars were the most carefully made-up. Everybody stood by. The wardrobe woman, the hairdresser, makeup man, they all were involved. They played soft music. Then, when you were in the mood to do it you posed. There was coffee, too, if you wanted it. And if you weren't going to work, you could have a drink. But *no more* is there anything like that. They just put up a set of lights and that's what everybody gets. Doesn't matter whether it's good for you or not. It's all such a rush now. It's all so money-minded, budget-minded. Nobody can take *time* anymore!

I wasn't very much involved in answering the fan mail during the early days. There was just too much of it! They had endless men and women taking care of it at the studio. And I would say to them sometimes, "Oh, that's a goodie. Make these up and send them to the fans.'' Then the people in the publicity department would just sign my name. They'd practice your signature! Then they'd sign for you. In the last ten years, I've done my own signing. Also during the war I insisted on signing for every soldier that asked for a photo. That took *hours!* They came so fast! I'm talking not about the Civil War but World War II [laughing]. I just wanted to get that straight. And you know, you'd get these wonderful lonely letters from the boys and I was very damn sure I wrote something personal to them.

When I was a kid and we came out of the moving picture show, as we called them then, I always felt like I was the leading lady. I took on her expressions and I became a different person walking away from that theatre. It was very exciting for me to be able to do it.

There were so many portraits of me in the Thirties, friends used to say to me, ''What the hell, do you own those movie magazines?'' I was on all the covers and inside for, oh, about ten years. That's a long time!

Back then, the photographers worked to get all kinds of flattering angles, moods, and so forth. They'd spend as long as two hours sometimes to light a genuine close-up for the motion-picture camera. The still camera went faster, of course. But do you know what it's like today! Well, *forget it!* They have guys come on the set, I think they pay them by the day or hour, and you can be sitting in the dark talking with the director, or in the middle of a sneeze or a cough and they'll just keep snapping away! And *none* of them will take out the ugly pictures!

I think glamour is the most important thing on earth. Reality and glamour go hand in hand. I think you have only half a job when there's just one of them. Reality is okay. We live it. But if you're in the cinema watching a film, so what if the girl's on the desert and her hair is flying. So what if she's been crawling on the desert for days. It can be in a *glamorous* way! A hairdresser works very hard to get that look and the cameraman has the wind machine blowing just right so the hair will softly cross her face. There's nothing wrong in that. It's show business we're in, remember. Not solely reality. We want to be entertained and we want to be thrilled when we go to the theatre or the movies. We want to have our dreams, too—don't we?

JOAN CRAWFORD. New York, January, 1972.

George Hurrell used to give me just one key light, and for him I never wore makeup. Just a scrubbed face. Hurrell loved photographing me without make-up—except for my eyes and lips, of course. He worked to catch you off guard. He'd talk to you constantly and his camera would go click, click, click, click, click while I was saying "Nooowwww," or "Reeeeeaaaallly." And he'd get pictures while I was talking, asking for a cup of coffee, whatever. I don't know if he did that with everyone else because many people are very conscious of the camera. I'm not.

Clarence Bull was a very quiet, serious man. He might joke with you before you started the sitting, but once you were in there he was the most dedicated man imaginable. Hurrell worked to keep you relaxed, but of course when Bull was photographing me I didn't know what relaxation meant. I didn't know to tease myself; I had no sense of humor. I was the "posy" type. That was something I overcame by developing a sense of humor about myself. I'd make fun of myself. But never other people, only myself. Also, I think you really have to feel in your heart before it shows here, on your face. In your eyes and around your mouth.

Richard Avedon gets me to move. He talks to me and gets exciting things from me. I play in front of his camera. Hurrell used to follow me, too. His camera was on wheels and he'd follow me around. How he used to move that camera, shoot the picture and move the key light with it, I'll never know! He looked like an octopus! But it all got there!

Adrian taught me so much about drama. He dressed me in black for the dramatic picture. He said *nothing* must detract. Everything must be simple, simple, simple. Just your face must emerge. No one should say, "Oh, isn't that a lovely collar," or "Oh; look at that necklace." "Aren't those earrings divine?" He made me conscious of the importance of simplicity.

This lovely portrait (page 125) was taken of me during what I called my "gardenia" stage. I loved gardenias. I wore gardenias everywhere. I had great bowls of gardenias all over my house. But unfortunately I'd have to throw them away about an hour after I'd put them on. They just turned brown. Nothing you can do about it. I just have too much body heat.

I've always answered my own fan mail. The autograph today is almost the same as it always was. I never used a stamp, either I know many stars who did, and I thought it was a bad practice. I *loved* posing in the gallery. It was hard work, but I loved it! I've always said my mother and father were both cameras. I've never known anything *but* a camera. That's why I'm so relaxed in front of them, I think.

Hurrell always played music. The later the hour, the gayer the music. To give you that lift. I loved torch songs, Crosby, Perry Como, Tony Martin. I was always sad listening to Bing Crosby's records.

I love being a celebrity. I never go out on the street unless I expect and anticipate and hope and pray that I'll be recognized. That someone'll ask for my autograph! When they do. I'm prepared and ready and as well-dressed as I possibly can be. And when somebody says, "There's Joan Crawford," I say, "It sure is!" And I'm very happy about it!

Glamour. That's what the movie business is, isn't it! Yes! Well, unfortunately, it isn't anymore. I've always said that glamour begins with cleanliness. Not makeup. Bathe first. That's number one with me. Glamour should never be superficial. It should be part of your habit, part of your life-style. I think to most people, glamour is just somebody who has nothing to do all day except bathe and oil their bodies and have massages and do nothing but look at themselves in the mirror and try different makeups. Well, I know many socialites who really have nothing to do but go to a salon and have a manicure and a pedicure. I have mine at my desk! Which reminds me, she comes tomorrow!

I've always kept changing throughout my career. I have a theory that a little bit of every part we play, if we like the character, rubs off on us. And we adapt and adopt it for our own personality. We don't know we're doing it. We have no idea we're taking it on. I think Katharine Hepburn took some of the character in *Bill of Divorcement* into her own life. At the time she did *Philadelphia Story* she took a part of that into her own personality. In his book *Four Fabulous Faces*, Larry Carr shows how Marion Davies, Gloria Swanson, everyone imitated my fuller mouth, darker eyebrows. But I wouldn't copy anybody. If I can't be me, I don't want to be anybody. I was born that way!

BETTE DAVIS. Westport, Connecticut, February, 1972.

Roman Freulich was the first portrait photographer to do a sitting with me when I got to California. When they looked at me, they called me 'the little brown wren', because with Harlow around, my hair was just mousey blonde. So they made me bleach it. They had me looking like everybody. They even made up my mouth like Garbo. Now I ask you, do you see anything like Garbo about me? After one year at Warner's I snuck down to Perc Westmore's salon and had it dyed back to my own color. A year later, Hal Wallis called me into his office and said. "You've dyed your hair back to its original color." That's all he said.

George Hurrell was the greatest! He took fantastic portraits of me. One as the girl in "Dark Victory" is the most wonderful picture of a tortured girl I've ever seen. He was brilliant. Bert Six at Warner's was good too, so was Frank Powolny at Fox, and Elmer Fryer. I'm reluctant to call any of them except Hurrell great, however, they were perfectly competent photographers. I must say I'm surprised looking at the early photographs of Elmer Fryer and Bert Six, how really sensational they are. In fact I've just changed my opinion about them. They were much better than good.

A new form of photography was started by Life Magazine. Their photographers started using the candid camera, which meant you never posed for them, and for the most part were unaware that they had taken a picture of you. This meant that the photographs taken in this way were less static. This method of photography to this day contributes most of the photographs from motion pictures.

The truth is in every field how many real artists are there? Even in the fashion magazines, how many are there taking definitive photographs? Avedon and Engstead are two that come to mind. I think a cameraman is a little like a doctor. The more sensitive he is, the easier it is to work for him. An actor is subject to many moods. In the portrait field, Hurrell, while photographing, was always able to make you re-live the part from the film you had just finished.

It's been twenty years since I've been in a still gallery after a film. Now all photographs are taken during the hours of shooting on the stage.

I've never been a film fan. But I've loved millions of performances. As a kid I saw Rudolph Valentino in the "Four Horsemen of the Apocalypse" about five times. I went to watch the scene where he kneels and takes off Alice Terry's shoes. I was mad for that one scene. I hoped one day some man would do the same for me. As for the other stars, I adored Garbo. I thought she was utterly fascinating. Katharine Hepburn too, I always admired her, always wished I looked like her!

I answer fan mail; I never send shiny prints or little studio prints. I send a large matt print. I have a painting of me done by an artist, Don Moore. I had it photographed and am now sending this to any requests for a photograph of me.

I just remembered that there was an extraordinary set photographer, not a gallery man, but a set-man working on "Of Human Bondage". He got some marvellous pictures of me. I'd go off in a corner and pose for him when we weren't filming. He was fantastic. I think his name was Alex—Alex Kahle!

Actually, I hated gallery photography, there was something static about it. It was not the photographer's fault, but it never felt natural to me. I was in no way fascinated with the camera; even the motion picture camera. Acting was the main thing. Hepburn was the same way. Glamour wasn't our bag!

ALEXIS SMITH. New York, December, 1971.

When I first signed at Warner Brothers in 1940, I was fresh out of college. The idea that they were going to transform me into a glamorous movie star never occurred to me, so I just did whatever the studio told me to do. It seemed as though the executives saw a certain quality in the actor and set about to create an image, and while they were creating mine, for the most part, I was just having fun.

My first portrait sitting with Elmer Fryer, then head of Warner's photo department, proved, I think, a great success. I loved his first portraits of me. They were quite dramatic and, I thought, lovely, because I always preferred portraits with dark backgrounds. This is probably my favorite studio portrait. (page 206).

Most of the portrait sittings were fun, but they were tiring, too. Usually, an entire day was spent doing nothing but posing. In my case, I'm afraid the photographers didn't particularly relish shooting me because they couldn't keep me still! Having been trained as a dancer I was always moving, and when they'd get me in the pose they wanted, I would move to another one before they could snap the shutter. I had too much energy just to sit quietly.

Everyone at Warner's was friendly with the photographers. I liked them all: Bert Six, Elmer Fryer, "Scotty" Welbourne, George Hurrell. Working with them was very easy and relaxed.

I must say, however, I never really related to the resulting glamour girl photographs. I knew they were photographs of me, of course, but I never really recognized them as myself. I think that's why the naturalistic photography today is so much more appealing. It gets so much closer to the truth.

The Twenties and Before

Theda Bara, 191

The Twenties and Before

From World War I until the great stock market crash in 1929, Americans were dancing to the Charleston, the Black Bottom and the Cakewalk; sporting "bee-stung" lips and flat chests; swooning to Rudolph Valentino's "sheik" and crying over Janet Gaynor and Charles Farrell as lovers in *Seventh Heaven*; buying the Model T Ford, raccoon coats and the phonograph; applauding the Ziegfeld Follies and George White's Scandals; praying for Charles Lindbergh and his *Spirit of St. Louis*; laughing at Chaplin, Keaton, Lloyd, Laurel and Hardy and Chester Conklin; imitating Joan Crawford, Norma Shearer, Gloria Swanson and Greta Garbo; paying $2.50 to see *Birth of a Nation* and *Intolerance*; singing "Over There," "Sweet Georgia Brown," and "Diane"; watching the nickelodeon give way to the gigantic movie palaces like the Roxy, the Palace, the Orpheum; writing millions of letters each year to America's Sweetheart, Mary Pickford; thrilling to the dancing of Vernon and Irene Castle; reading the newspapers of William Randolph Hearst; believing Louella Parsons as she reported on Hollywood; making popular authors of Anita Loos, F. Scott Fitzgerald, Fannie Hurst, Edna Ferber and Sinclair Lewis; hailing the discovery of penicillin by Sir Alexander Fleming in 1928; welcoming the talking picture; reading Edna St. Vincent Millay's poetry; glorifying the It girl; swimming in one-piece bathing suits; buying Tiffany lamps; cheering Babe Ruth's sixty-homerun record; applauding Katharine Cornell; making *Abie's Irish Rose* a long-running Broadway hit for 2,327 performances; and amending the Constitution to prohibit the sale of liquor and to give women the right to vote.

Anna Q. Nillson, 1920

Rudolph Valentino, 1924

Constance Talmadge, 1922

Harry Langdon, 1928

opposite Corinne Griffith, 1924

Buddy Rogers, 1927

opposite Mary Brian, 1925

Rod La Rocque, 1923

opposite Joan Crawford, 1928

Joyce Compton, 1928

Walter Pidgeon, 1929

John Wayne, 1929

Betty Bronson, 192

Ilie Burke, 1917

Charles Farrell, 1928

opposite Janet Gaynor, 1927

Charles Chaplin, 1918

opposite Alice Joyce, 1919

above Madge Bellamy, 1925

left Betty Blythe, 1920

opposite Charles Ray, 1927

Nazimova, 1922

Gloria Swanson, 1918

opposite Gloria Swanson, 1921

Barbara LaMarr, 1925

opposite Francis X. Bushman, 1926

above Evelyn Brent, 1928

right Leatrice Joy, 1922

opposite Pola Negri, 1921

opposite Clara Bow, 1928

right Gloria Swanson, 1916

below Helen Bray, 1916

opposite Carole Lombard, 1929

Carole Lombard, 1926

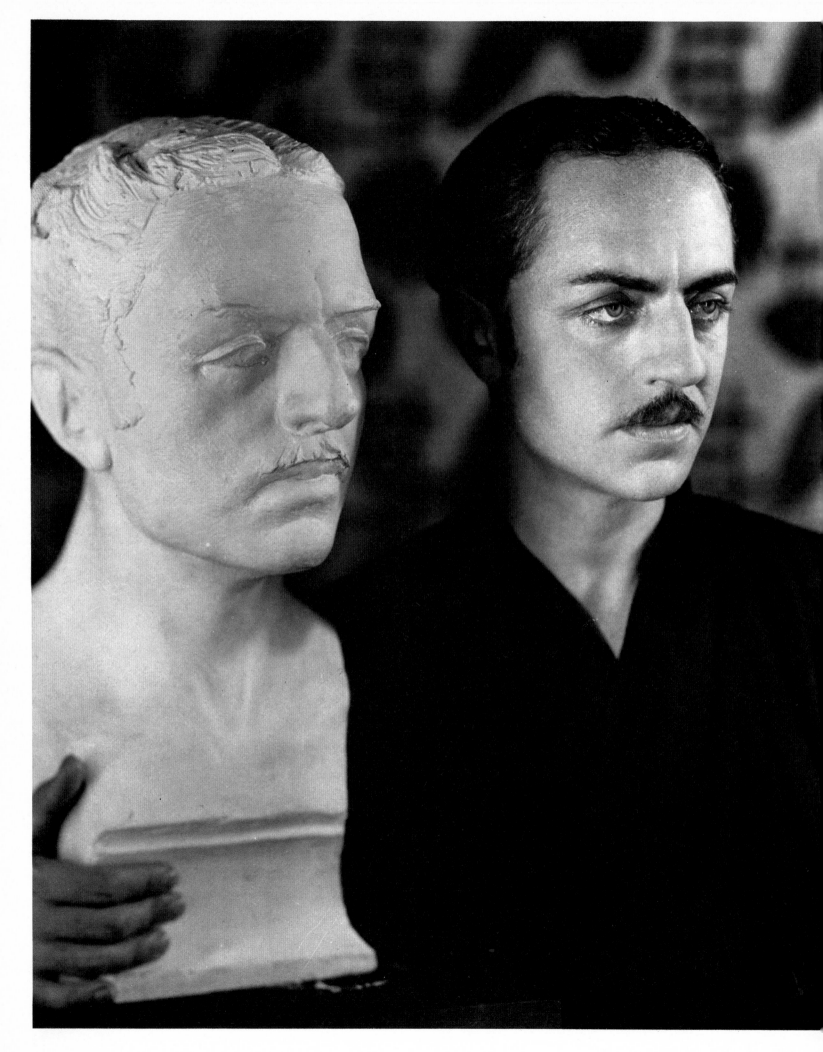

Mae Murray, 1924

opposite William Powell, 1928

Dorothy Gish, 1926

Lillian Gish, 1926

Lillian Gish, 1924

opposite Richard Barthelmess, 1928

Mary Miles Minter, 1918

opposite Elsie Ferguson, 1919

Gary Cooper and Colleen Moore, 1928

opposite Gary Cooper, 1929

opposite Mae Busch, 1922

Joseph Schildkraut, 1929

opposite Wallace Reid, 1921

Mabel Normand, 1918

Norma Talmadge, 1922

Nils Asther, 1928

Ronald Colman, 1926

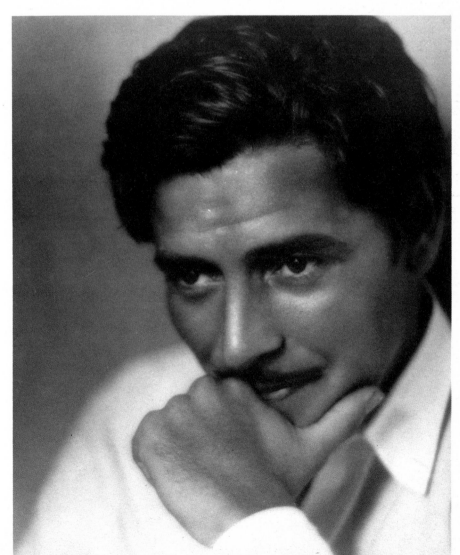

Opposite Greta Garbo, 1929

opposite Dolores Costello, 1926

Mary Astor, 1926

Marion Davies, 1917

The Thirties

The Thirties

From the stock market crash in 1929 until the beginning of World War II in Europe, Americans were singing the tunes of George Gershwin and Cole Porter; laughing at the comedy of the Marx Brothers, Mae West and W.C. Fields; screaming in fright at *Frankenstein, Dracula,* and *King Kong;* crying at *Wuthering Heights, Gone with the Wind,* and *Stella Dallas;* electing Franklin D. Roosevelt to the Presidency; thrilling to *Snow White and the Seven Dwarfs* and *The Wizard of Oz;* buying the records of Bing Crosby, Rudy Vallee, Kate Smith and Ethel Merman; applauding Bette Davis in *Dark Victory,* Katharine Hepburn in *Bill of Divorcement,* Clark Gable and Claudette Colbert in *It Happened One Night,* and Spencer Tracy in *Captains Courageous* and *Boys' Town;* reading *The Ladies' Home Journal, The Woman's Home Companion, Collier's* and *Delineator;* following the trials of "Little Orphan Annie"; believing Orson Welles' "War of the Worlds" was real; dancing the Carioca; making matinee favorites of Jean Harlow, Clark Gable, Errol Flynn, Olivia de Havilland, Barbara Stanwyck and Robert Taylor; attending Busby Berkeley's musicals starring Ruby Keeler, Dick Powell and Joan Blondell; grabbing movie magazines as soon as they hit the newsstands; loving Shirley Temple; making popular stars of Fred Astaire and Ginger Rogers as they danced and romanced in *Top Hat, Flying Down to Rio,* and *Follow the Fleet;* disbelieving the 102 stories of the Empire State Building; standing on breadlines and putting their faith in the New Deal; and cheering the precision of the Radio City Music Hall's Rockettes.

opposite Tallulah Bankhead, 1932

Jean Harlow, 1934

Olivia de Havilland, 1936

Errol Flynn, 1935

opposite Maureen O'Sullivan, 1934

Lew Ayres, 1930

122

above Lana Turner, 1938

left Jean Parker, 1934

opposite Henry Fonda, 1935

Joan Crawford, 1935

Joan Crawford and Franchot Tone, 1933

opposite Joan Crawford, 1931

opposite Clark Gable, 1935

Carole Lombard, 1934

John Barrymore, 1934

Ethel Barrymore, 1932

Marie Dressler, 1930

Wallace Beery, 19

Warner Baxter, 1930

above Joan Blondell, 1935

left Dick Powell, 1938

opposite Alice Faye, 1935

Joan Bennett, 19

Robert Young, 1932

Ann Harding, 1936

Mary Astor, 1937

Melvyn Douglas, 1937

above Bette Davis, 1939

right Bette Davis, 1936

opposite Bette Davis, 1934

opposite Barbara Stanwyck, 1931

right James Stewart, 1937

below Spencer Tracy, 1933

138

opposite Paulette Goddard, 1936

left Buster Crabbe, 1933

below Diana Wynyard, 1933

above Marlene Dietrich, 1930

left Marlene Dietrich, 1937

opposite Marlene Dietrich, 1934

Aline MacMahon, 1932

Francis Lederer, 1934

uise Rainer, 1936

opposite Johnny Weissmuller, 1932

Dorothy Lamour, 1938

Merle Oberon, 193

Greta Nissen, 1933

Joan Fontaine, 1936

Fred MacMurray, 1938

Richard Cromwell, 193

Phillips Holmes, 1932

Randolph Scott, 19

Joel McCrea, 1933

Tyrone Power, 1936

Loretta Young, 1938

opposite Margo, 1937

left Anna May Wong, 1937

below Jane Wyatt, 1937

Barbara Stanwyck, 1936

opposite Gary Cooper, 1931

Ronald Colman, 1931

Brian Aherne, 1933

Ray Milland, 1939

George Brent, 1935

Mae West, 1933

Gwili Andre, 1933

Carole Landis, 193

Claudette Colbert, 1933

Margaret Sullavan, 193

Ida Lupino, 1936

Ann Sheridan, 1938

Louise Hovick (Gypsy Rose Lee), 1937

Miriam Hopkins, 1931

Katharine Hepburn, 1933

Charles Laughton, 1933

Elsa Lanchester, 1935

opposite Buster Keaton, 1933

Greta Garbo, 1931

opposite Greta Garbo, 1937

Charles Farrell and Janet Gaynor, 1934

Richard Arlen, 1930

opposite Fredric March, 193

Billie Burke, 1936

Ruby Keeler, 1933

opposite Jean Arthur, 19

Cary Grant, 193

Gladys George, 1936

Norma Shearer, 1939

Anna Sten, 1934

Nancy Carroll, 1933

above Gloria Swanson, 1933

right Virginia Bruce, 1936

opposite Myrna Loy, 1934

above Kay Francis and Herbert Marshall, 1932

left Betty Grable, 1938

opposite Dolores Del Rio, 1939

John Boles and Shirley Temple, 1935

The Forties

The Forties

From the beginning of World War II in 1939 until the end of the Forties, Americans were fighting in Europe, Asia and Africa; trying to recover from the shock of Pearl Harbor and Hiroshima; making Broadway hits of *Oklahoma!*, *South Pacific, Brigadoon* and *Annie Get Your Gun*; singing "Don't Sit under the Apple Tree with Anyone Else but Me" and "White Christmas"; swooning to Frank Sinatra, Perry Como and Bing Crosby; dancing to the music of Harry James, Xavier Cugat, Glenn Miller and Artie Shaw; collecting pinups and Petty girls; listening to "Dr. Kildare," "Lux Hollywood Theatre" and "The Romance of Helen Trent" on radio; supporting the stardom of Ingrid Bergman, Jennifer Jones and Lana Turner; electing F.D.R. and Harry Truman to office; wearing Maybelline, shoulder bags, lampshade hats, strapless bras, leg makeup and nylon dresses; buying war bonds; reading *The Fountainhead, Forever Amber* and *The Keys of the Kingdom*, escaping in Esther Williams movies and lavish M-G-M musicals starring Judy Garland, Kathryn Grayson, Van Johnson, Margaret O'Brien, Jane Powell, Jose Iturbi and Jeanette MacDonald; laughing at Jimmy Durante, Abbott and Costello, Judy Canova and Joe E. Brown; making Gorgeous George and wrestling national favorites; listening to the screams of bobbysoxers; awaiting *The Outlaw*; discovering new playwrights Arthur Miller and Tennessee Williams; enjoying the dancing of Gene Kelly and Fred Astaire; gasping at Dior's "new look"; loving *The Best Years of Our Lives, Mrs. Miniver, Gentlemen's Agreement, The Song of Bernadette*, and *National Velvet*; and thinking turbans and snoods were absolutely the last word.

above Ann Sheridan, 1941

left Ann Sheridan, 1940

opposite Ann Sheridan, 1941

opposite Patricia Neal, 1949

right Joan Blondell, 1947

below Eleanor Parker, 1946

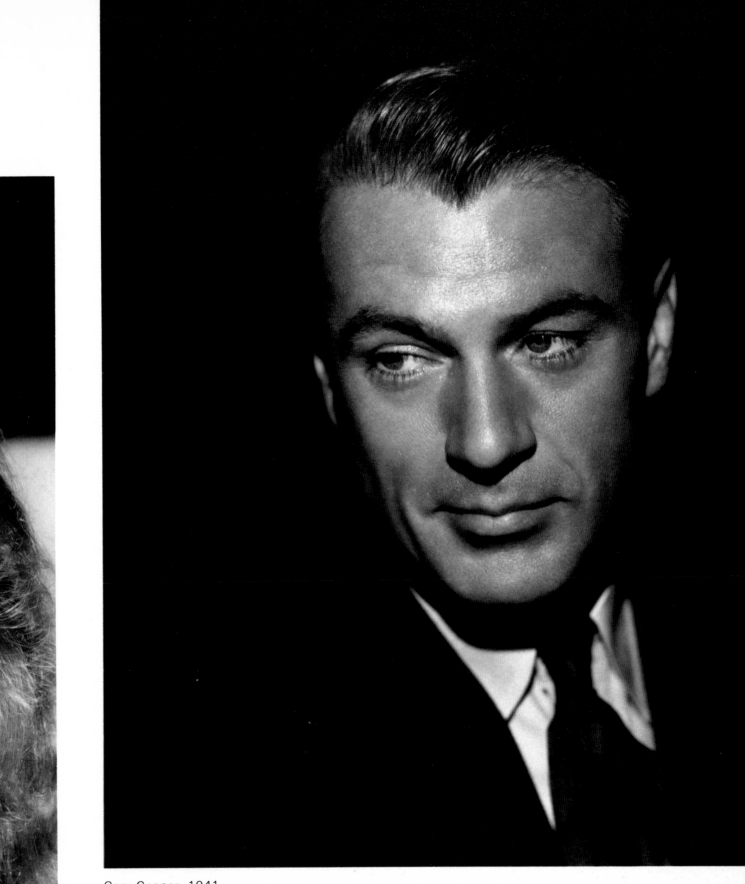

Gary Cooper, 1941

Ingrid Bergman, 1942

left Lilli Palmer, 1946

below Elisabeth Bergner, 1941

Robert Taylor, 1942

opposite Lana Turner, 1940

above Hedy Lamarr, 1940

left Hedy Lamarr, 1940

opposite Hedy Lamarr, 1946

Clark Gable, 1945

Olivia de Havilland, 1947

above Gloria Swanson, 1941

right Marta Toren, 1948

opposite Ann Sothern, 1940

above Veronica Lake, 1942

left Veronica Lake, 1941

opposite Veronica Lake, 1941

Brenda Marshall and William Holden, 1945

Barbara Stanwyck and Gary Cooper, 1941

opposite
Spencer Tracy and Katharine Hepburn, 1945

above Rita Hayworth, 1944

right Rita Hayworth, 1940

opposite Rita Hayworth, 1941

Madeleine Carroll, 1940

opposite Sterling Hayden, 1941

opposite Vivien Leigh, 1941

right Robert Preston, 1940

below Laurence Olivier, 1940

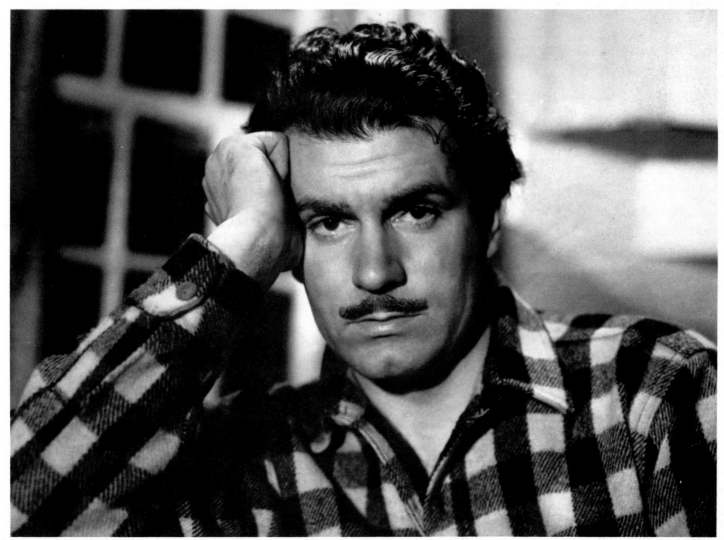

Alexis Smith, 1946

Jane Greer, 1945

opposite Constance Bennett, 1940

Fred MacMurray, 1942

opposite Rosalind Russell, 1940

Gene Tierney, 1941

Anne Baxter, 1941

opposite Jeanne Crain, 1945

opposite Ava Gardner, 1947

right George Sanders, 1947

below James Mason, 1949

left Susan Hayward, 1941

below Greer Garson, 1941

Claude Rains, 1940

opposite Bette Davis, 1941

Maureen O'Hara, 1940

Glenn Ford, 1946

John Garfield, 1940

Betty Field, 19

Deborah Kerr, 1947

opposite Betty Hutton, 1943

Ginger Rogers, 1942

Judy Garland, 1943

Joan Crawford, 1942

opposite Humphrey Bogart, 1943

Rita Hayworth, 194

John Wayne, 1949

Bette Davis, 1947

Barbara Stanwyck and David Niven, 1947

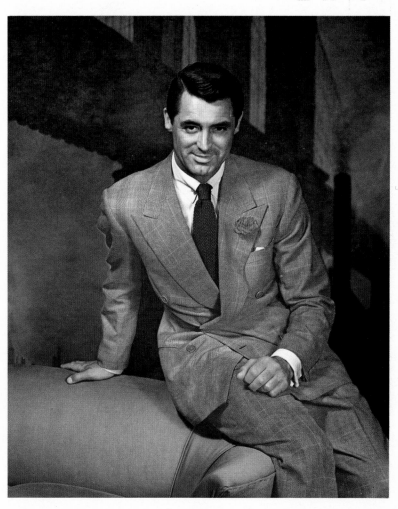

Cary Grant, 1943

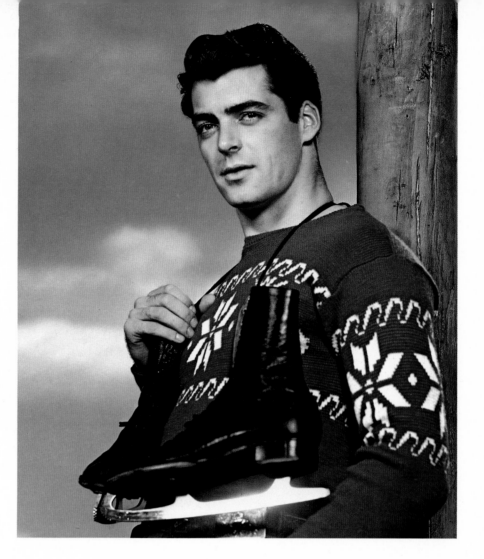

Rory Calhoun, 1947

Gregory Peck, 1948

opposite Lana Turner, 1946

230

Tyrone Power, 1947

Maria Montez, 1944

Susan Hayward, 1942

Ray Milland, 19-

Deanna Durbin, 1947

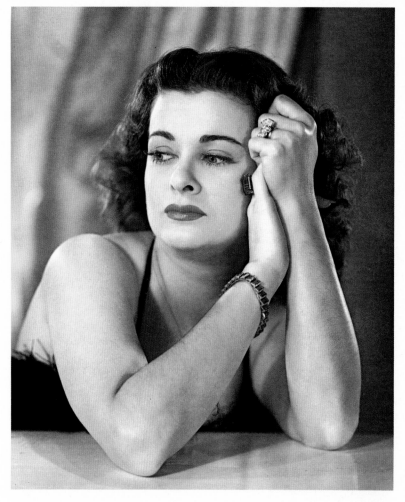

Joan Bennett, 1945

Jane Wyman, 1946

Jennifer Jones, 1946

The Fifties

The Fifties

From the beginning of the Fifties when soldiers were fighting in Korea, until 1959 when John F. Kennedy was campaigning for the Presidency, Americans were singing "All I Want for Christmas Is My Two Front Teeth," "Come On 'a My House," and "Autumn Leaves"; laughing at Amos and Andy, Sid Caesar, Imogene Coca, Phil Silvers, "I Love Lucy," Milton Berle, Martha Raye and "I Married Joan"; dancing to rock and roll, the music of Fats Domino, Chuck Berry and Little Richard; loving Elvis Presley; buying records for hi-fi sets; wearing leather jackets, crew cuts and argyles; electing Eisenhower to office—twice; watching Elizabeth crowned Queen of England; fussing with crinolines; enjoying seamless stockings and the poodle cut; reading *Peyton Place*; copying Marilyn Monroe's walk; making idols of James Dean and Marlon Brando; admiring Kim Novak's beauty; bidding goodbye to Grace Kelly who became a foreign princess; rebelling against authority; digging the jazz at New York's Birdland; playing with the hoola hoop; crowding into phonebooths and Volkswagens; riding motorcycles and motor scooters; living in pre-fabricated houses; moving to the suburbs; admiring Suzy Parker in *Vogue*; liking *Quo Vadis, Cat on a Hot Tin Roof, Bridge on the River Kwai, On the Waterfront*, and *East of Eden;* being amused by 3-D, Cinerama and CinemaScope; discovering the excitement of Stan Kenton's jazz, Miles Davis' trumpet, and June Christy's voice; attending Broadway hits *My Fair Lady* and *Long Day's Journey into Night;* watching the "$64,000 Question," Jack Paar, Steve Allen, Loretta Young, Arlene Francis, Alfred Hitchcock, "Playhouse 90," and "Armstrong Circle Theatre"; criticizing beatniks; and being shocked and challenged by the Russian Sputnik.

posite Kim Novak, 1955

Grace Kelly, 1955

opposite Marlon Brando, 1950

Montgomery Clift, 1953

Richard Boone, 1951

Farley Granger, 1955

Richard Basehart, 19

Mitzi Gaynor, 1951

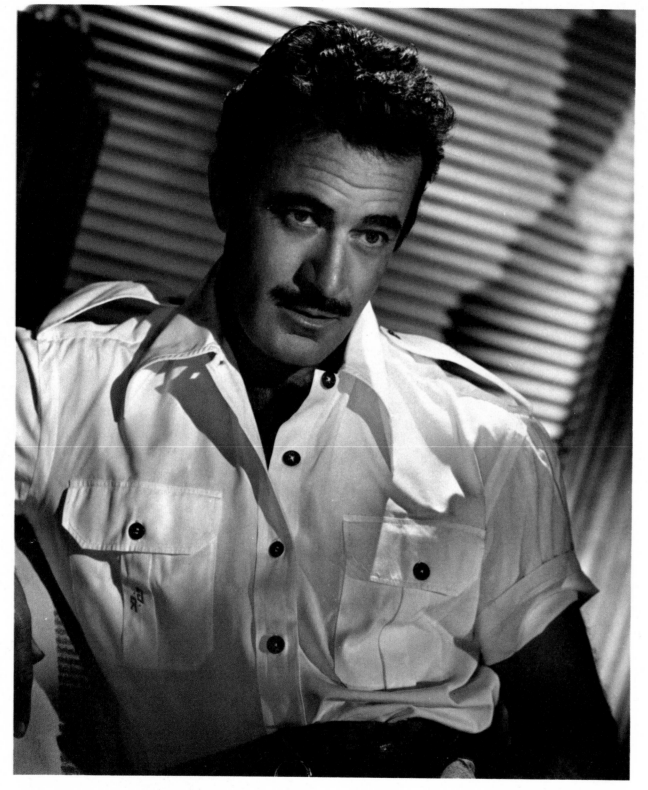

Gilbert Roland, 1953

opposite Joan Crawford, 1952

opposite Robert Mitchum, 1956

left Hardy Kruger, 1958

below Anita Ekberg, 1958

opposite Tab Hunter, 1958

following page Marilyn Monroe, 1958

Hildegarde Knef, 1951

William Holden, 1953

Louis Jourdan, 1951

opposite Audrey Hepburn, 1954

Jeff Chandler, 1958

opposite Lana Turner, 1958

James Mason, 1951

opposite Judy Garland, 1954

Elizabeth Taylor, 1952

opposite James Dean, 1955

Arlene Dahl, 1959

Anne Baxter, 1950

opposite Cary Grant, 1958

Marlene Dietrich, 1951

Gertrude Lawrence, 1950

opposite Gloria Swanson, 1952

Lex Barker, 1953

John Ireland, 1955

opposite Ruth Roman, 1951

opposite Burt Lancaster, 1951

right Susan Hayward, 1957

below Rita Hayworth, 1952

Robert Taylor, 1951

opposite Bette Davis, 1955

Richard Burton, 1953

Jean Simmons, 1953

opposite Sophia Loren, 19

above Paul Newman, 1959

right Rock Hudson, 1956

opposite Kim Novak, 1956

rilyn Monroe, 1958

ht Clark Gable, 1956

posite Tony Curtis, 1956

The Sixties

The Sixties

From the election of John F. Kennedy in 1960 throughout the "do your own thing" Sixties, Americans were screaming at the Beatles, the Stones, Paul Revere and The Raiders, The Doors, the Dave Clark Five and The Association; loving Richard Chamberlain as Dr. Kildare and Vince Edwards as Ben Casey on television; listening to hard rock, folk rock and folk music; reading Jacqueline Susann and Harold Robbins; paying attention to the words of Dr. Martin Luther King; noticing the behavior of Timothy Leary, Abbie Hoffman and the Black Panthers; being hijacked in jumbo jets to Cuba; learning that cigarettes were definitely hazardous to health; attending Broadway productions of *Hello Dolly, Fiddler on the Roof* and *Who's Afraid of Virginia Woolf;* landing astronauts on the moon; requesting the music of Henry Mancini, Burt Bacharach and Hal David; reading Ian Fleming and seeing James Bond films starring Sean Connery; facing a severe drug problem among the nation's youth; tuning in Huntley and Brinkley; watching "Peyton Place" on television; dancing the Twist and the Frug; experimenting with marijuana; beginning to take women's liberation as a serious issue; following the escapades of Richard Burton and Elizabeth Taylor; queuing up for *Woodstock, 2001: A Space Odyssey, The Graduate,* and *The Sound of Music;* buying high fashions at the flea market; wondering about LSD; copying Jacqueline Kennedy's dress and hair styles; hearing new words pollution and ecology; sending Shirley Temple to the UN; and trying to understand the assassinations of two Kennedy brothers and Dr. Martin Luther King.

opposite Peter O'Toole, 1966

Albert Finney, 1967

opposite Audrey Hepburn, 1967

278

opposite Mia Farrow, 1964

left Warren Beatty, 1964

below Clint Eastwood, 1969

above Vanessa Redgrave, 1967

left Julie Christie, 1967

opposite Alan Bates, 1970

Dean Stockwell, 1960

opposite Wendy Hiller, 1960

284

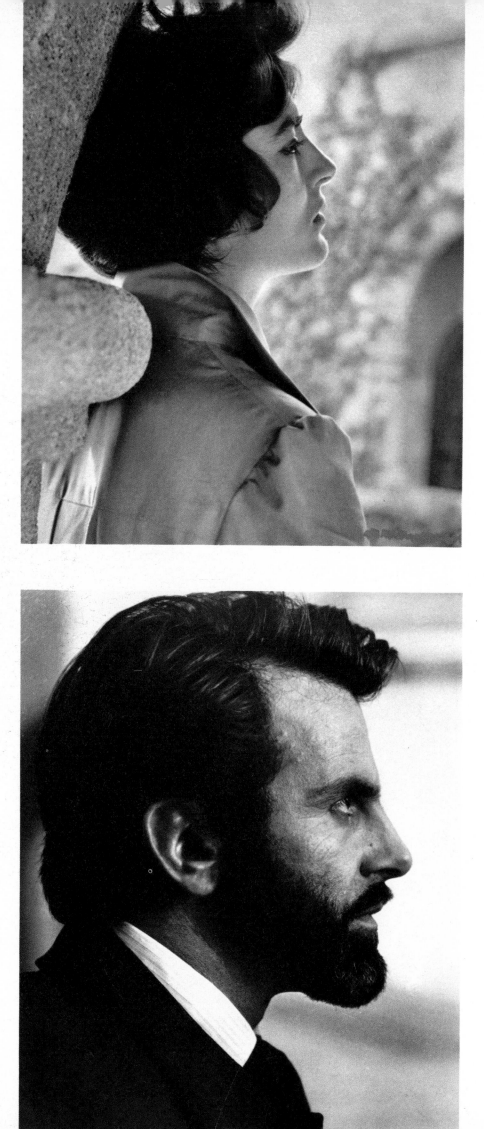

Irene Papas, 1961

Maximilian Schell, 1970

opposite Elliott Gould, 1970

Sophia Loren, 1966

Romy Schneider, 1963

opposite Marlene Dietrich, 1961

Alain Delon, 1964

Britt Ekland, 196

Sondra Locke, 1970

Gregory Peck, 196

andice Bergen, 1968

opposite Anthony Perkins, 1962

right Robert Shaw, 1969

below Melina Mercouri, 1964

above Natalie Wood, 1961

right Paul Scofield, 1967

opposite Capucine, 1967

Lana Turner, 1960

Barbara Stanwyck, 1963

opposite Joan Crawford, 1964

Ingrid Thulin, 1970

Genevieve Page, 1964

opposite Susan Hayward, 196

opposite George C. Scott, 1967

Julie Andrews, 1968

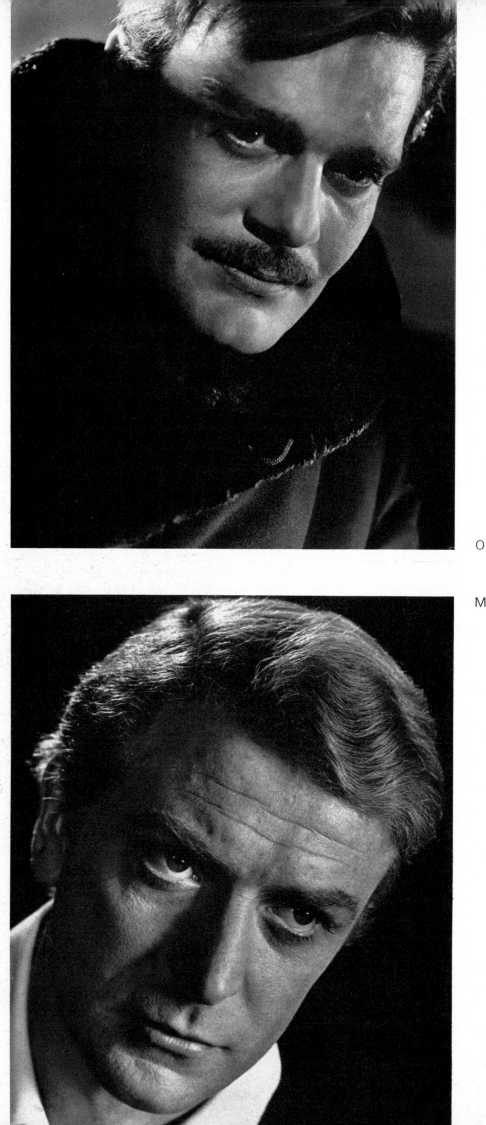

Omar Sharif, 1965

Michael Caine, 1968

opposite Anouk Aimee, 1969

opposite Elizabeth Taylor, 1968

Richard Burton, 1963

right David Hemmings, 1967

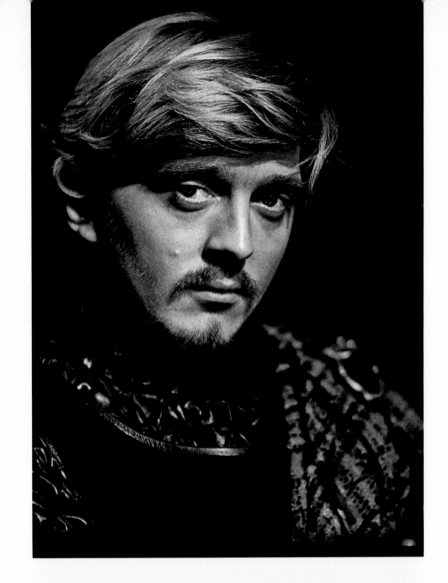

above Katharine Hepburn, 1968

below right Helmut Berger, 1970

right Samantha Eggar, 1969

below Barbra Streisand, 1970

above Ann-Margret, 1964

right Candice Bergen, 1968

opposite Terence Stamp, 1966

Charlton Heston, 1965

below Sharon Tate, 1967

Steve McQueen, 1966

right Anna Magnani, 1969

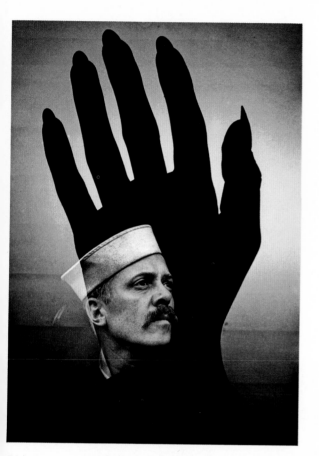

Richard Attenborough, 1966

below Ursula Andress, 1965

Raquel Welch, 1968

Jane Fonda, 1962

Lauren Bacall, 1965

The Photographers

The following is a list of portrait photographers and studios whose work appears in this book—photographer credit is given only when positive identification was possible: James Abbe, Kenneth Alexander, Ted Allen, Max Munn Autrey, Ernest A. Bachrach, Russell Ball, Frank Bez, Milton Brown, Clarence Sinclair Bull, Malcolm Bulloch, Campbell Studios, Eric Carpenter, Robert W. Coburn, Schuyler Crail, Carl DeVoy, Otto Dyar, Don English, John Engstead, Tom Evans, Charlotte Fairchild, William A. "Bud" Fraker, Roman "Jack" Freulich, Elmer Fryer, Louis Goldman, Milton Greene, Norman Hargood, Edwin Bower Hesser, Hoover Art Studio, Hoppe Studio, George Hoyningen-Huene, George Hurrell, David James, Ray Jones, Doug Kirkland, Irving Lippman, Kenneth C. Lobben, Bert Longworth, Ruth Harriett Louise, Mandeville Studio, Charles Moore, Fred Morgan, Hans Namuth, Hal Phyfe, Frank Powolny, Rice Studio, Eugene Robert Richee, Sarony Studio, Fredric Walter Seeley, A. L. "Whitey" Schafer, Emmett Schoenbaum, Jack Shalitt, Bert Six, Melbourne Spurr, W. E. Thomas, Peter Turner, Underwood and Underwood Studio, William Walling, Jr., George Courtney Ward, Scotty Welbourne, Lazlo Willinger, Witzel Studio.

Index

Index of portraits, by star, year, photographer (only when positive identification was possible), film studio or company that released portrait, film title of approximate time portrait was taken (General Publicity when no title was available), page. The following is a list of abbreviations used for film studios and releasing companies:

Col, Columbia
FN, First National
Nat Gen, National General
Para, Paramount
20th, 20th Century-Fox
UA, United Artists
Univ, Universal
WB, Warner Brothers

Acknowledgements

We are grateful to the following for their assistance in the preparation of this book: Academy of Motion Picture Arts and Sciences; Irving Adler, Paramount Pictures; Jerry Anderson, 20th Century-Fox; Marie Baxter, *Look* Magazine; Catherine Benevento; Miss Joan Blondell; Beverly Brumm; Ralph Buck, United Artists; James Card, George Eastman House; Bernadette Carozza, *Photoplay* Magazine; Larry Carr; Kathleen Carroll; Dorothy Chase; Bill Christy; Buddy Clayton; Miss Joan Crawford; Ken Cunningham, *Photoplay* Magazine; Miss Bette Davis; Miss Olivia de Havilland; Victor de Keyserling; Patty Ecker, Cinerama Releasing Corporation; Elizabeth Eblen; Margaret Eversole; William K. Everson; Barry Fishel, 20th Century-Fox; Monroe Friedman, Universal Pictures; Joseph Fusco, 20th Century-Fox; Jack Goldstein, Allied Artists; Lou Gross; Kyra Hackley; Hannah Henner; Jose Hernandez, 20th Century-Fox; Cornelia Hice; Betty Hill; Iris and Tibor Hoffman; Herb Honis, United Artists; Ted Hooks; George Hurrell; Bob Jackson; Saul Jaffe; Stephen Johnston, Walter Reade Organization; Norman Kaphan, M-G-M; Jack Kerness, Columbia Pictures; Helen Killeen, United Artists; Jack Lyons, Paramount Pictures; Lou Marino, Warner Brothers; Leslie Martinson; Eric Nauman, Universal Pictures; Doyle Nave, International Photographers of the Motion Picture Industry, Hollywood; Vivian Sexton Newman; Ruth Pologe, American International Pictures; George C. Pratt, George Eastman House; Bobbie Mason Rawlings; Dorothy Reynolds; Alan Rogers, 20th Century-Fox; Carole Rosenberg, National General Pictures; Jonas Rosenfield, Jr., 20th Century-Fox; Peggy Rosenthal, Cinema V; Jeanne Sams; Mary Scher; Harold Schiff; Miss Alexis Smith; Ted Spiegel, Avco Embassy Pictures; John Sutherland, Warner Brothers; Nancy Tester; Vivian Tibbetts, Warner Brothers; David Toser; Lou Valentino; Paula Vogel, Columbia Pictures; Leo Wilder, Warner Brothers; Hernando Wilson, 20th Century-Fox.